INTRODUCTION

BEWARE THE FULL MOON!

A full moon lights up the night sky. OWWWHHH! A howl fills the air. It strikes fear into the bravest heart. Watch out! A werewolf is on the hunt for human flesh!

A werewolf is a man or woman who turns into a wolf when there is a full moon. By night, a werewolf is a savage monster. It kills and eats anyone or anything it meets. By day, it is human again.

If you're lucky, the only werewolves you'll see are in movies and books. But hundreds of people say real werewolves have attacked them!

Werewolves are feared all over the world. In South America, a wolfman called a lobizón eats babies and animal dung. In Germany, boxenwolves hunt for horses to eat.

Do these terrifying monsters really exist? Read on and decide for yourself...

TALES OF HORROR

WEREWOLVES

Jim Pipe

ticktock

TALES OF HORROR
WEREWOLVES

Acknowledgements

Copyright © 2006 *ticktock* Entertainment Ltd.

First published in Great Britain by ticktock Media Ltd.,

Unit 2, Orchard Business Centre, North Farm Road, Tunbridge Wells, Kent TN2 3XF, Great Britain.

All rights reserved. No part of this publication may be reproduced, stored in a retrieval system, or transmitted in any form or by any means electronic, mechanical, photocopying, recording or otherwise, without prior written permission of the copyright owner.

A CIP catalogue record for this book is available from the British Library.

ISBN 1 84696 013 4 Printed in China.

Picture Credits:

t=top, b=bottom, c=centre, l=left, r=right, OFC=outside front cover, OBC=outside back cover.
Acclaim Images/Cathy McKinty: 4/5 (main pic). Amit Gogia CyberMedia Services: 6/7, 10/11 (main pic). Corbis: 22/23 (main pic), 27 (main pic). c.20thC.Fox/Everett/RexFeatures: 26tl. ShutterStock: 1, 10tl, 17cr, 18/19 (main pic), 20/21 (main pic), 20bl, 22tl, 24bl, 28/29 (main pic), 28bl, 30/31 (main pic), 31tl, Kurt De Bruyn 8-9 (main pic), Mindy w.m. Chung 8/9 (main pic), Norma Cornes 16/17 (main pic), Jaimie Duplass 21cr, Wendy Kaveney Photography 8bl, Magdalena Kucova 13tr, Micah May 25, Bridget McPherson 12/13 (main pic), Robert C. Tussey III 16bl. ticktock Media image archive: OFC, 5tr, 6tl, 14/15 (main pic), 14tl, 15tl, 18tl, 23tl, 30tl.
Every effort has been made to trace the copyright holders and we apologize in advance for any unintentional ommissions.
We would be pleased to insert the appropriate acknowledgement in any subsequent edition of this publication.

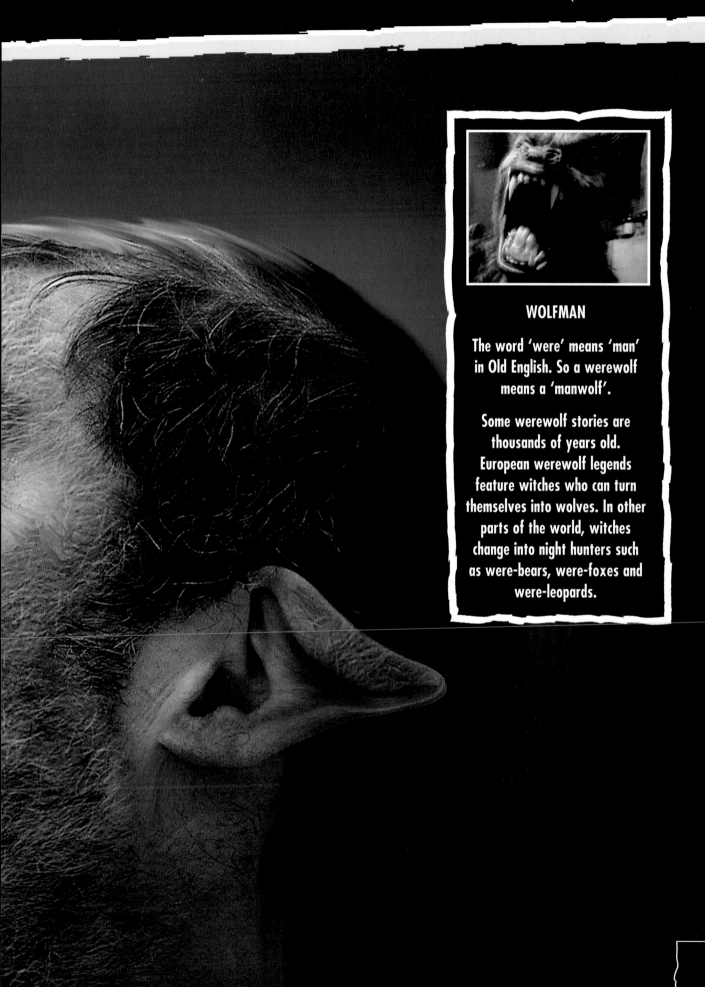

WOLFMAN

The word 'were' means 'man' in Old English. So a werewolf means a 'manwolf'.

Some werewolf stories are thousands of years old. European werewolf legends feature witches who can turn themselves into wolves. In other parts of the world, witches change into night hunters such as were-bears, were-foxes and were-leopards.

FROM MAN TO WOLF

Bones crack, muscles grow. A giant jaw with long fangs bursts from his mouth. Thick, dark hair sprouts all over his body. Claws spring from his toes and fingers. Man has become wolf!

It's not all fun being a werewolf! Okay, so you become bigger, faster and stronger. But changing from a man into a monster really hurts!

In some reports, werewolves look half-wolf, half-human. In early Native American legends, wolfmen walked on all fours. In later legends, they began walking upright to become more human. Many of the wolfmen seen in Europe also walk on two legs.

In other stories, werewolves are more like giant wolves. They run on all fours. Their bodies are covered in silver fur. Their red eyes glow like burning coals in the dark.

"Niceros tells of a friend who stripped off his clothes and hailed (howled at) the stars... all at once he became a wolf... Niceros heard that a wolf had been worrying cattle and had been wounded in the neck. On his return home, he (Niceros) found his friend bleeding at the neck, and he knew that his friend was a werewolf..."

From *Satyricon* a book by a Roman writer called Petronius, written about 2,000 years ago.

THE CURSE OF THE WEREWOLF

You wake up in a field, miles from home. Your clothes are torn. There is blood all over your hands and face. You have a terrible headache and you can't remember anything from the night before. Hmmm… sounds like you're a werewolf!

Do you want to be a werewolf? The smart answer is no!
So, you need to avoid:

- Being bitten or scratched by another werewolf.
- Eating the flesh or brains of a wolf.
- Drinking water from a wolf's paw print.
- Swimming in a cursed stream (in Greece).
- Being born on Christmas Eve (in Italy).

Actually, most people cursed with being a werewolf don't like it. They feel terrible about killing other people. But they can't help it. Some werewolves try to kill themselves to be rid of this curse. Watch out, though. A few do enjoy having the superhuman strength and speed of a werewolf. They also love the taste of human flesh!

WOLF MAGIC

German werewolves are called boxenwolves. They change into wolves by putting a magic strap around their body. Horses are their favourite food. In one German village, a man was paid to whisper magic words into the ears of horses each night. The words protected the horses against the boxenwolves.

9

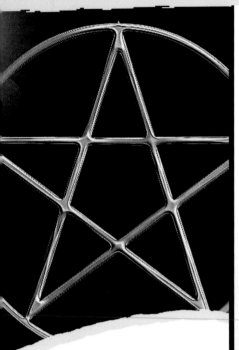

HOW TO SPOT A WEREWOLF

Do your friends have...
a) rough hair on their palms?
b) an extra long index finger?
c) really thick eyebrows that meet in the middle?

TELL-TALE SIGNS

Some werewolves have tattoos of the moon on their body. Others are marked with a pentagram. This five-point star is an ancient magic symbol. A werewolf may see a shadow of this star on the forehead of its next victim.

Russian werewolves have hair under their tongue. They also have blood-red fingernails and a small tail hidden under their clothes!

If so, they might be a werewolf! There are other ways to spot a werewolf. Werewolves have very bad breath and terrible BO! Some werewolves are even said to have purple pee.

A werewolf's habits can give it away. Many werewolves avoid running water, such as rivers and streams. Werewolves also hate light. In some legends they can't even look up at the sky.

Are your neighbours always replacing their pets? It may be a sign that they are eating them. When there's a full moon, you may also be kept awake by howling from next door.

Finally, watch out for someone who hangs around graveyards. They may be a werewolf looking for freshly buried bodies to munch on.

KILLING A WEREWOLF

The werewolf snarled as it backed into the corner. The hunter aimed his pistol. A single bullet sped from the gun, through the heart of the monster. The werewolf was dead.

In old movies, only a silver bullet can kill a werewolf. In 1767, the Beast of Gevaudan (a French werewolf) was shot and killed with a silver bullet made from a holy cup.

However, any weapon that kills a normal wolf will kill a werewolf. So shotguns, spears, traps or poison will all work. In the 17th century, the Catholic Church preferred two methods. The first was to cut off the werewolf's head with a double-edged sword. The second was to stab it between the eyebrows with a pitchfork!

Once your werewolf is dead, cut off its head, burn the body and scatter the ashes. Now the werewolf's curse is broken. That means anyone once bitten by this werewolf becomes human again.

WANT TO BE A WEREWOLF HUNTER?

Are you mad? Finding a werewolf before it changes is hard. During the day, it behaves like everyone else. It has the brains of a human, so traps won't fool it.

If you find a werewolf after it's changed, try and hurt it. A wound will show up when it turns back into a human. In its human form a werewolf is weaker. Be warned, some werewolves hunt in packs. Help!

THE FIRST WEREWOLVES

A man walks to the edge of a lake. He hangs his clothes on a tree, and then plunges into the water. When he appears on the far side of the lake, he is a wolf!

Members of a secret religion in Arcadia, ancient Greece, believed that jumping into a lake would change them into a wolf. They could only become human again if they had not eaten human flesh for nine years. In 400 BC, a member of this group, Damarchus, won a boxing match at the Olympics. It is said he changed into a wolf during the fight.

Werewolves are as old as story telling. The *Epic of Gilgamesh*, written four thousand years ago, features Enkidu. He is a werewolf-like hairy man.

In an ancient Greek myth, King Lycaon of Arcadia chops up his grandson. Then he serves the body to the god Zeus. When Zeus finds out he punishes Lycaon, by turning him into a werewolf.

"They were like wolves, but their faces were small and long... and they had great ears. The skin on their spine looked like that of a pig. In some villages they ate more than 100 people... These monsters entered houses... they climbed in the night onto terraces, and stole children from their beds."

Werewolves in Iraq described by the writer Denys of Tell-Mahre, around AD 770.

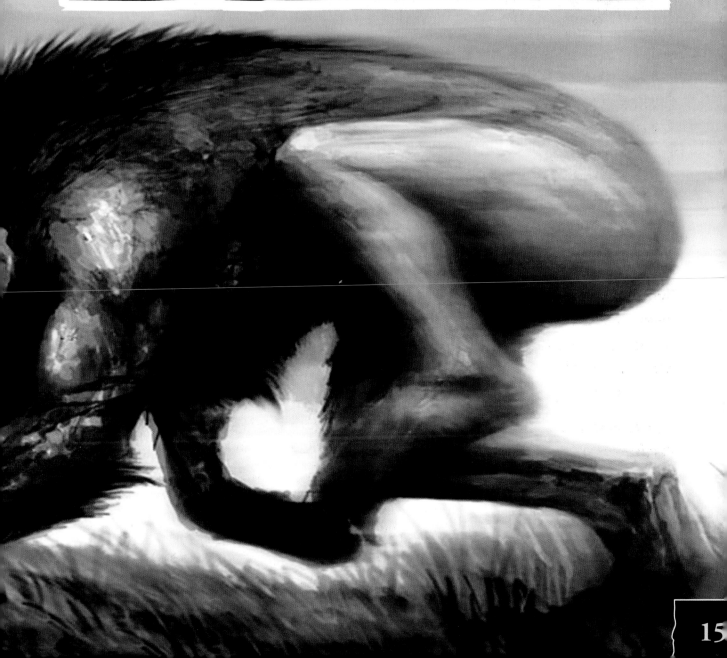

A CURSED TOWN

There are many werewolf tales from the Middle Ages.
In the 12th century, historian Gerald of Cambridge tells of
an Irish priest who meets a talking wolf.

The wolf begs the priest to visit his dying wolf wife. The wolf tells
the priest that St Natalis has cursed the town of Ossory, in Ireland.
Every seven years, two people from the town must put on wolf skins
and turn into werewolves. When the priest visits the dying she-wolf,
she peels off her fur. Underneath is the skin of an old woman.

THE GREAT WEREWOLF HUNTS

t is 1439. One summer's evening, a pack of hungry wolves runs silently though the streets of Paris. In a single night, they kill and eat 14 people.

In the Middle Ages, people saw wolves as evil killers. In 1300, the town of Vicenza in Italy built new walls as protection against werewolves! In Germany and Serbia, anyone found guilty of being a werewolf had their head cut off and their body burnt.

In Europe, the Church spread the idea that witches could turn into wolves. Many people believed it was true. From 1520 to 1630, some 30,000 people were killed for being werewolves. They were accused of stealing cattle and killing children. Many people admitted to being werewolves after being horribly tortured.

In Italy, people believed that werewolves grew thick hair inside their skin. Several suspects died after being cut open by doctors.

BUCKLES, BELTS AND BULLETS

In the year 1640, in the town of Griefswald, Germany, many people were dying. It was thought that werewolves were responsible. A group of students decided to take action. They melted down silver buckles and belts to make strong silver bullets. With these bullets, the students were able to shoot the werewolves.

THE BEAST OF GÉVAUDAN

On the night of 15th January, 1765, a man struggles through the snow, looking for his son. He sees a shape on the ground. Coming closer, he gasps in horror at the bloody body lying on the ground…

The man, Pierre Chateauneuf, brought his son's body home and sank into a chair. He claimed that he looked up and saw a werewolf's glassy eyes staring at him through the window. Grabbing his musket, Pierre fired at the monster. But it ran off.

This werewolf became known as the 'Beast of Gévaudan'. People said it had thick, dark hair and an evil smell. In three years, the beast killed over 60 people in the mountains of south-central France. Whole villages were deserted as people fled in terror.

MONSTER OR MYTH?

Several hundred men finally hunted down the Beast of Gévaudan. It was shot with a silver bullet through the heart.

There were rumours that the actual beast was too horrible to show in public. So, the body of a large wolf was carried through the streets.

But was the beast really a werewolf, or just a wolf?

WERE-CREATURES

A beautiful woman walks into the room. But something isn't right. Is that a tail hidden under her clothing? You happen to see her reflection in a mirror – she's a were-fox!

Humans that turn into beasts are in stories from all over the world. In Indian folklore, people change into were-tigers and were-foxes. In Russia they become were-bears, in Peru were-jaguars. In Chile there are witches who turn into chonchons, a mix of vulture, lion and human.

The Santu sakai are were-monsters from Malaysia, called 'mouth men'. They have large fangs and love the taste of human flesh. These monsters attack remote villages, killing and eating their victims.

The Berber peoples of Morocco believe in boudas, sorcerers that turn into hyenas. Real hyenas can make a sound just like a human voice. So are these were-monsters all in the mind?

WERE-FOXES

Were-foxes are very popular in the legends of China and Japan. Unlike werewolves, they do not start out as humans. In China, a fox that lived for 500 hundred years could change into a human!

The Japanese were-fox, called a kitune, is usually female. Its bushy tail can be seen, even when it's in human form. A kitune turns back into a fox at night. It plays tricks on people.

SHAPE-SHIFTERS

A medicine man dances and chants to the rhythm of a drum. The drum beats faster. The man goes into a trance. He calls out to the spirits, "Now I am an eagle upon your winds, soaring high into the clouds!"

In many cultures there are stories of gods and people changing into animals. This power is known as shape-shifting.

The Navajo Native American people of the southwestern United States tell stories about 'skin-walkers'. A skin-walker is a healer who uses magic to change into an animal such as a wolf, bear or eagle.

In Iceland, a hamrammr is a were-creature that changes into the animal it has just eaten. Its strength increases with each animal it gobbles up.

In Mexican folklore, the nahual are witches who turn into wolves, jaguars or eagles. They do this to attack their enemies. The nahual do not like blades, scissors, piles of grey ash or garlic.

BIG, BAD WOLF?

Native Americans have always looked kindly on 'Brother Wolf'. They respect a wolf's hunting and tracking skills.

A wolf provides food for all its family, including the old and sick members of the pack.

Wolves once followed the herds of bison that moved across the Great Plains of North America, just like the Native American hunters.

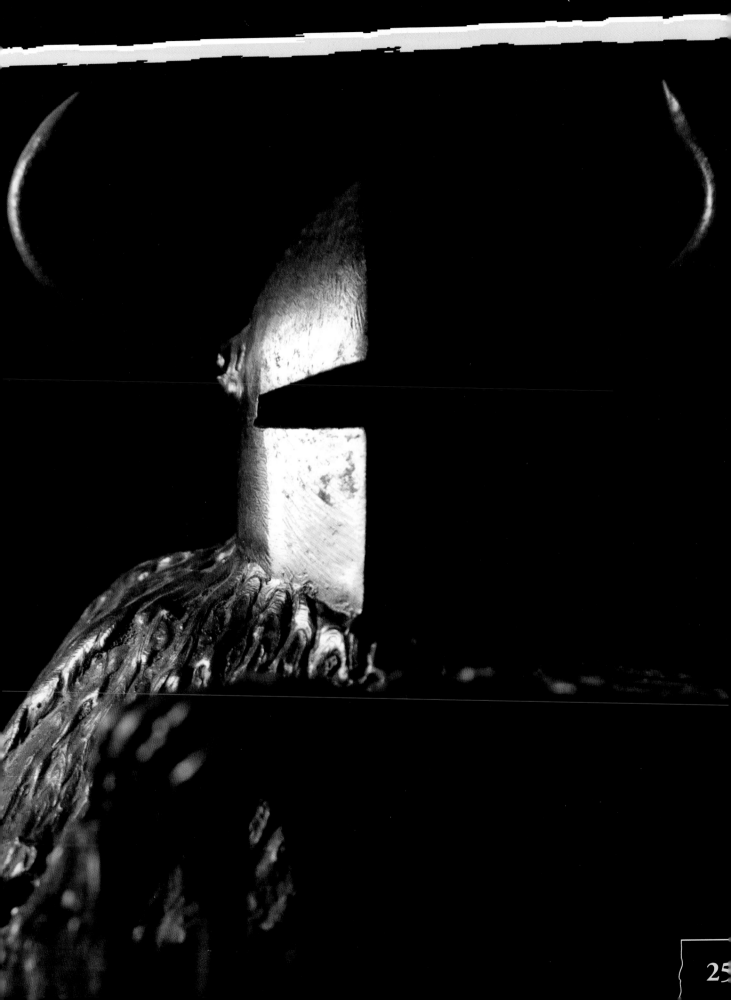

MOVIE WEREWOLVES

"Even he who is pure in heart, And says his prayers by night, Can become the wolf when the wolfbane blooms, And the moon is full and bright." (Ancient rhyme, used in the movie *The Wolf Man* in 1941).

CAT PEOPLE

There are many movies with were-creatures. In *Cat People* (1942), a beautiful women turns into a black panther. In *The Fly* (1958), a scientist turns into a giant fly after an experiment goes horribly wrong.

Comic book characters also take on the powers of an animal. In the movie *X-Men* (2000), Wolverine is a wolf-like superhero with sharp blades on the ends of his fingers.

Werewolves have been scaring movie goers for almost 100 years. In 1913, the silent movie *The Werewolf* used a real wolf as a werewolf! Later movies, such as *The Wolf Man* (1941), used an actor with hairy make-up. In recent movies, such as *Van Helsing* (2004) and *Brotherhood of the Wolf* (2003), the werewolves are created by computer graphics.

In the TV series, *Buffy the Vampire Slayer*, Buffy's friend Oz is a werewolf. When he is about to turn into werewolf, he gets his friends to lock him up. If they don't have time, they shoot him with a drug. Then Oz sleeps off his rage.

In *Teen Wolf* (1985), Michael J. Fox plays a teenager who uses his wolf powers to become the star player on the basketball team!

WEREWOLF OF L

WOLF WORSHIP

Where do werewolf stories come from? In the past, many warriors wore animal skins because they believed the skins would turn them into good fighters. Wearing skins also made them look like scary monsters!

In medieval Germany, people believed that great warriors became wolves when they died. Boys were called Wolfbrand and Wolfgang to make them strong and brave, like a wolf.

Viking warriors called Berserkers wore bearskin shirts. They believed the shirts would make them fierce and strong like a bear.

Before a battle, the Berserkers prayed to the Viking war god, Odin. Then they worked themselves into a fury. The warriors then charged into the fight, howling like animals. No wonder people thought they were being attacked by were-bears!

THE LEOPARD MEN

The Leopard Men were a secret society in West Africa. Local chiefs paid them to kill their enemies. They believed a magic drink made from their victim's stomach turned them into leopards.

A Leopard Man wore the skin of a leopard and an iron bracelet fitted with dangling knives. When he clenched his fist, the knives became claws.

DO WEREWOLVES EXIST?

It is 30,000 BC. In a dark cave lit only by torches, a caveman dabs red colour on the wall. He grunts happily. He has painted two-legged human figures – with animal heads!

People have reported sightings of werewolves for thousands of years. But do they really exist? One explanation for the sightings might be the disease rabies. People are bitten by an animal with rabies, may act like a wolf and become wild and froth at the mouth.

Most werewolves are probably people with a mental illness. In 540 BC, King Nebuchadnezzar of Babylon went mad for four years. He thought he was a wolf and let his hair grow wild. Some forms of madness can make people violent or very strong.

During the 16th century, most people who admitted they were werewolves had been tortured into it. People accused others of being a werewolf because they didn't want to be accused themselves!

RARE DISEASES?

Some werewolves may be people with a condition known as hypertrichosis. This makes you incredibly hairy.

Another rare disease, porphyria, also makes people look like a werewolf. Their skin changes colour, thick hair grows on their face and they become sensitive to light.

Beserkers Viking warriors who worked themselves into a mad frenzy before battle. The word comes from berserk, which means to go mad.

Executed To be killed as a punishment.

Medieval A period in history from about 1000 - 1453.

Monastery A building where monks live.

Musket A long gun.

Pentagram A five-pointed star that can be drawn in a continuous line. Pentagrams are believed to be magical.

Pitchfork A long-handled tool with thin prongs. It is used for lifting and moving hay or straw.

Saga An ancient Viking story, often about heroes.

Shape-shifters People who can turn themselves into an animal. Often a sorcerer.

Sorcerer Someone who practises magic, such as a witch or wizard.

Superhuman Having incredible powers or strength, much greater than ordinary humans.

Tattoo A coloured ink pattern on the skin made by pricking the skin with a thin needle.

Vampire A supernatural creature that feeds on the blood of its human victims.

Were-creatures Humans that turn into animals, often predators (hunting animals), such as leopards, tigers or wolves.

Werewolf A man or woman that turns into a wolf when there is a full moon.

Wolfsbane A plant that is said to protect against werewolves.